# BELLA

## AN UNSOLVED MURDER

# BELLA

## AN UNSOLVED MURDER

*Joyce M. Coley*

**HISTORY INTO PRINT**

First published by
History into Print, 56 Alcester Road,
Studley, Warwickshire B80 7LG in 2007
www.history-into-print.com
Reprinted October 2007
Reprinted January 2012

ISBN: 978 1 85858 315 0

A Cataloguing in Publication Record
for this title is available from the British Library.

Typeset in Plantin
Printed in Great Britain by
SupaPrint (Redditch) Limited

# INTRODUCTION

Ten years ago I became very interested in an unsolved murder in war time Hagley. I vaguely remembered hearing about it as a child but it was only when looking it up to write an article for the Fircone Magazine of the writers group in Birmingham that I discovered there was a mystery still surrounding the murder.

I still search for any relevant information and it has become quite a hobby. After giving a talk to a W.E.A. group in Dudley, I was put on the speakers' list and since then have talked to many groups. I was really surprised at the interest shown and this was increased after the television programme in September 2005 Inside Out with Matthew Gull.

The money from the talks helps many charities and I have bookings well into 2008.

My thanks to all who have helped and given encouragement over the years.

Mrs Joan Slater, the Birmingham writer who started it all.

Mr Robin Skerratt, the nephew of Sergeant Skerratt who gave encouragement and loaned books.

Mrs Carol Hodgson of Clent History Society for much information and help.

Matthew Gull for the programme and video.

Andrew Bullas for copies of his work and other papers.

Judith O'Donovan for her knowledge of Claverley and Jack Mossop.

The many people who allowed me to interview them.

To Mrs Lyz Harvey the leader of the Clent Writers for so much help in bringing this book to its conclusions.

And to all those who listened to the talks and gave their ideas too.

# Bella – An Unsolved Murder

## 60 years after the murder

### HAGLEY VILLAGE

Hagley a lovely Worcestershire village 20 miles from Worcester is well known for its links with history. The seat of the Lytteltons, Hagley Hall, the last mansion built in the Palladian Style sits elegantly in its famous parkland, visited by the rich and famous since the Georgian Days and well known from the family connections with the gunpowder plot. Around the park lies dense woodland, the home of many deer and the site of the well remembered murder. Beautiful with its elegant houses and farmsteads, it was anything but peaceful at the time of the murder. Many strangers were living in the village or passing through at a time of dire threat to the country early in the war.

Evacuated mothers and children filled the spare rooms of houses and increased the numbers in the village school. A detachment of the Welsh Regiment was billeted in the next village Pedmore and they walked around the woods and park with girlfriends or took part in exercises in the area. An Ack Ack battery was sited in the nearby Field House and the skies were alight every night from nearby searchlights. Some of the workforce from the wartime site at Hartlebury were billeted in the village. An R.A.F. station in the Furlongs farm picked up signals and deflected enemy bombers from their path to Coventry and Birmingham. Tired men, at work all day, walked around at night time carrying out duties as Home Guard or Firewatching. People were weary, frightened and hungry for food was limited and fuel was scarce. Anyone from the cities who could find some fuel used the village as a bedroom to sleep away from the bombing in vehicles parked along lanes and in lay-bys.

# A DIFFICULT MYSTERY TO SOLVE

In 1943 the village policemen were given a very difficult task. They were determined that no crime should remain unsolved on their patch. With only bicycles for transport and a great deal of extra work due to the war, it is amazing how much work they did with the resources at their disposal.

The crime was discovered in 1943. Four boys who lived in Lye often walked to the Clent Hills at weekends. A favourite jaunt, they brought their lurchers Trix, Jock and Nigger in the hope of catching rabbits to eke out the rations.

They were Bob Hart, from Pearson Street, Bob Farmer from Balds Lane, Fred Payne from Stocking Street and Tommy Willetts the youngest. Fred was unwell and died later from kidney disease, but the two older boys still remember the day they found the tree.

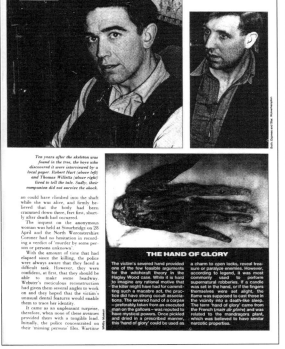

**DISCOVERY**

Ten years after the skeleton was found in the tree, the boys who discovered it were interviewed by a local paper. Robert Hart (above left) and Thomas Willetts (above right) lived to tell the tale. Sadly, their companion did not survive the shock.

an could have climbed into the shaft while she was alive, and firmly believed that the body had been crammed down there, feet first, shortly after death had occurred.

The inquest on the anonymous woman was held at Stourbridge on 28 April and the North Worcestershire Coroner had no hesitation in recording a verdict of 'murder by some person or persons unknown'.

With the amount of time that had elapsed since the killing, the police were always aware that they faced a difficult task. However, they were confident, at first, that they should be able to make some headway. Webster's meticulous reconstruction had given them several angles to work on and they hoped that the victim's unusual dental features would enable them to trace her identity.

It came as an unpleasant surprise, therefore, when none of these avenues provided them with a tangible lead. Initially, the police concentrated on their 'missing persons' files. Wartime

**THE HAND OF GLORY**

The victim's severed hand provided one of the few feasible arguments for the witchcraft theory in the Hagley Wood case. While it is hard to imagine any rational motive that the killer might have had for committing such a macabre act, the practice did have strong occult associations. The severed hand of a corpse – preferably taken from an executed man on the gallows – was reputed to have mystical powers. Once pickled and dried in a prescribed manner, this 'hand of glory' could be used as a charm to open locks, reveal treasure or paralyze enemies. However, according to legend, it was most commonly used to perform supernatural robberies. If a candle was set in the hand, or if the fingers themselves were set alight, the flame was supposed to cast those in the vicinity into a death-like sleep. The term 'hand of glory' came from the French (main de gloire) and was related to the mandragora plant, which was believed to have similar narcotic properties.

*Above: Bob Hart.*

There is little cover on the hills and no rabbits wished to be caught on that day so with a feeling of disappointment they tried to get some excitement by returning through Hagley woods knowing that if they were caught trespassing they would be punished.

They began to look for birds' eggs. A hazel tree which had been coppiced so many times that the trunk looked rotten stood in the wood. About five feet from the ground was a black hole and from the base many shoots had grown. Bob thought that it was a likely place for a blackbird to nest. He climbed up and looked down into the hollow trunk.

Something light coloured was lying down inside. As it was impossible to reach he cut a branch and hooked the object up on the end of it.

As it fell onto the ground they realised with horror that it was a skull. "Is it from a fox?" asked the youngest boy. "No it looks like a human skull to me" said Bob. They all knew that this was a serious matter which they should report, but if they did they would get into trouble for trespassing in the woods. That would bring punishment when they got home and they might not be allowed to go out at weekends in future. They must put it back where they found it. Bob tried but the skull would not stay on the stick. In desperation he picked up some of the rotten material and making a wedge in the jaws pushed it onto the stick and lobbed it back into the hollow tree. They swore each other to keep the secret.

The boys ran for home but one boy was so frightened by the experience that he broke his word and told an adult. Perhaps the boys were wrong but someone had better make sure for it was unlikely that the frightened youngster could have made it up. The man went to discuss it with his friend the local police sergeant in Lye, Chris Lambourne. They decided that the eldest boy should take them to the tree on the next day for them to make sure about the matter. Bob Hart was angry, "that Tommy Willetts has opened his big mouth, we could be sent to court for poaching." Reluctantly he showed the men the rotten tree. The men could see the skull and a bone sticking up with some decayed material but it was enough to denote a crime scene. The local Police were informed. Sergeant Skerratt of Clent and P.C. Pound of Hagley came to the wood. No-one could touch the evidence until the C.I.D. had been called from Worcester. The forensic scientist was Professor James Webster, the most famous man of his day with a track record of solving most crimes, but it would take 24 hours to bring him with his team and the scene could not be left unguarded.

Volunteers were sought to stay in the wood for the night but there was no mad rush of willing people.

Fortunately a young man who was awaiting his call up to the R.A.F. had been in the specials since 1940. His name was Douglas Osborne and he was brave enough to volunteer. Later he had a distinguished career in the war and he was always interested in the mystery.

*P.C. Richard Skerratt.*  *Centre: Eric Douglas Osborne.*

# SEARCHING FOR EVIDENCE

Professor Webster, Superintendent Sidney Inight and Det. Inspector Tom Williams arrived the next day. The hole in the tree was approximately five feet from the ground and fairly narrow so they could not reach the remains. Jack Pound, a lumberjack in his youth, fetched his axe and almost decimated the rotten tree, until every particle could be removed. With the skull they found some

bones, a cheap wedding ring...the type bought in Woolworths which had been worn for about 4 years, a bottle, a pair of crepe soled shoes and some rotten material. Seeing the jaws stuffed with material, Webster at first thought that she had committed suicide. Most of the skeleton was missing, probably carried away by the woodland animals.

Webster believed that the most valuable evidence was found at the scene of the crime. Many helpers were brought in to work

through the woodland to find the remaining bones. Scouts, Home Guard and others came to carefully search among the bluebells. Most of the skeleton was found but there was one unusual find. The right hand was discovered complete at about thirteen paces from the tree, whereas the other small bones were randomly dispersed.

From this macabre discovery many of the stories relating to witchcraft gathered pace in the village.

Cleverly Webster reconstructed most of the skeleton but there was no real evidence of violence. He deducted that she had been dead from 18 months to 2 years. Her height was around 5 feet and she had given birth to a child. She was not a manual worker and she had had a tooth extracted in the twelve months before her

Something white grinned up at them from that gloomy gap in the bar. Something with teeth and eye-sockets. Something dead and nightmarish.

'It's a human skull', one blurted out.

'No - it's an animal's', insisted his pal.

'Might be a dog's or a fox's, more like', declared the eldest of the four.

Despite this assurance, the Wych Elm had suddenly become a place of dread and the joys of that spring bird-nesting expedition were replaced by nagging uncertainty. They hastily left the spot and headed for home. Tommy Willetts, the youngest member of the bird-nesting gang, was still certain that the skull they had discovered was human. The matter still continued to trouble his mind and he told his father as much, that night.

But for Mr Willetts' presence of mind, 'Bella' might yet be lying in that crumbling coffin of a tree. Next morning, he reported his son's suspicions to Sgt. Charlie Lambourn (then in charge of Cradley). He immediately telephoned Sgt Dick Skerratt at Clent and arranged to meet him, with the bird-nesting quartette at

with the rotting remains of a cotton garment. His quick pronouncement that they were involved in a case of 'Murder by suffocation' came as no surprise to the experienced detectives who surrounded him.

A further careful examination revealed the rest of the skeleton, in a sitting position at the back of the tree's hollow bole. It was obvious that the skull had toppled off and rolled into the centre of the cavity. To the side of the cranium which had been in contact with the ground, a whispy 'pelt' of sodden hair was still attached.

squads of volunteers to help comb the undergrowth in ever-widening circles from the exact scene of the crime.

Dick Skerratt recalled that when the day's task was completed it was the habit of those involved to adjourn to 'The Gypsy's Tent' (a nearby hostelry) for refreshment. Inevitably, the main subject of conversation was the search in which they had been willing participants and many ingenious theories were put forward by 'amateur tecs' in those well-lubricated sessions.

The professionals present mostly listened in amused silence but P.C. Jack Pound

this refusal to complete the conundrum stemmed from self-preservation.

### More Info. on Skeleton

Professor Webster's painstaking work continued and he was able to confirm that the skeleton was, indeed, that of a female, aged about 35.

He also concluded that she had given birth to one child, had been about five-feet in height and that she had not been a manual worker. Her hair colouring was 'mousey' and one of her teeth had been extracted during the year prior to her death. He considered that she had been dead for between one and four years but his most calculated estimate was about 18 months.

Perhaps the most telling clue the skull provided was the singular manner in which the front incisor teeth were 'crossed'.

This information prompted a nation-wide police enquiry. Practically every dentist in the country was contacted and it was, at first, thought that this avenue of investigation would be fruitful, owing to the very unusual formation of the victim's teeth and the fact that she had undergone dental treatment in the year before

death. She had a distinctive formation of the front incisors which were crossed. This would have made her appearance noticeable.

Her clothing was also reconstructed and she had been wearing a woollen skirt and cardigan, a pink petticoat and blue panties, with black crepe soled shoes. A picture of her was circulated although they had no facial evidence in the hopes that someone would recognise her.

They questioned everywhere for any happenings in 1941 which may have been of significance. The police remembered an incident when two men were out walking in the woods and reported screams. They had tried to trace the cause themselves unsuccessfully. The police investigated the area but also found nothing. They assumed that perhaps the men had heard the cry of a vixen which can have a human quality.

Now the long hard work of the police began, made much more difficult in a time of war. 3,000 missing women over 1,000 square miles were investigated but no-one fitted her description.

They were confident that the dental records would help to identify her but after a search of thousands of records they again drew a blank.

During this time the police received a letter from a soldier who stated that his girl friend Mary Lee was missing and probably in danger. His letter was backed up by one from his padre and another from his friend. After a long search they managed to find the lady. Mary liked changes and was by then with her fourth man and had changed her name. The police had been used by her former lover to find her.

A local man offered his help and after standing by the tree took himself home and put himself into a trance. The name and address of a woman he saw was checked by the police but there was no woman in existence with that name.

An identity card was found in the wood with the name and address of a woman from a town some distance away. This clue was also pursued. The woman was not aware that her card was missing and she had never been to, or heard of, Hagley Wood. There was no further work on how her card came to be placed there.

The clothing did not help as surprisingly there were no labels in any of the garments, not even the corsets.

NOTICEABLE IRREGULARITY FRONT TEETH, LOWER JAW

BROWN HAIR

HEIGHT ABT. 5 FT.

DARK BLUE STRIPED KNITTED WOOLLEN CARDIGAN

LIGHT BLUE BELT

AGE ABT. 35

MOCK WEDDING RING (VALUE 2/6)

CLOTH SKIRT WITH ZIP

PEACH COLOURED TAFFETA UNDER SKIRT

BLUE, CREPE SOLED SHOES

# THE SHOES

Their main hopes rested on the shoes. These were manufactured by Silesbys of Northhampton. 6,000 pairs had been produced and, to their credit, they traced the sales of all but six pairs. These had been sold on a market stall. One lady had swapped a pair of hers with a poor woman who had come to her door needing shoes. She had exchanged them for a pretty cup and saucer but did not know where the woman had come from. Later on in the search for clues the matter of the shoes comes up again in the story and the colour and nature of their description is altered.

## GYPSIES

Local gossip suggested that it was probably a gypsy killing. The woods were well known as a place for encampments. The local hostelry was then called THE GYPSIES TENT. The dangerous main road to Halesowen was known to have been cursed by the mother of a child who ran out from the camp and was killed. There have been many fatal accidents near the woods. The Police searched for anyone who had camped in the woods but there were no missing women to report.

## COVENS

The other stories grew from the fact that covens do meet around the area and she may have been a witch. From medieval times the hand of glory has been kept to make spells. The right hand of murderers was often kept for this purpose in times gone by. Some were taken from the victims hanging on the gallows. Another old practice was to put the bodies of dead witches into trees to keep their evil from working after their death. Many villagers would not walk near the woods after dark. Even Lord

Cobham said that he would not do so and they were his woods. The trail was getting cold and the local police were worried that after all they may have an unsolved crime on their patch.

## WHO PUT BELLA DOWN THE
## WYCH ELM – HAGLEY WOOD?

In 1944 there was another development. The message was found chalked in letters four inches high along a wall in Upper Dean Street, Birmingham. Soon the message was appearing in other places on bridges and walls around the Black Country area.

Had someone returned to the area who knew who she was? Maybe a serviceman returned from the front.

Again the police searched through thousands of missing persons looking for names like Isabella, Luebella, Claribella etc. all to no avail. Once more the trail was cooling.

## THE HOME GUARD

Later the police did get a story from Mr Basterfield who, before his call up, had been a member of the Home Guard. In 1941 whilst awaiting his call up papers he was on duty in a scout hut in Halesowen. They were turned out to investigate a parachute alert. With a friend he was patrolling Hagley Wood Lane. The drop had been on the Clent Hills and they were to question anyone in the area and close it off. A car was parked in the lay-by opposite the gate into the wood. There were often vehicles there as it was used by people from the towns who came out to get some rest from the bombing. An airman was sitting at the wheel and a woman was lying under a greatcoat on the passenger seat. She made no attempt to sit up. Thinking that perhaps she was with a lover and feeling shy they went to the driver's window. The man in officers uniform held up his card to the window. They told him to move on and when they returned the car had gone.

Many German Aircraft were bombing aircraft factories in Coventry and Birmingham then. The harness to the parachutes was found on the hills but not before someone had removed the silk, as it was a favourite material to make underwear.

## THE MAN WHO SAW BELLA

Whilst I was looking for the details of the mystery I asked for help from anyone who may know or remember the murder. The journalist of the County Express remembered the story and gave me the number of a man he had interviewed who had seen Bella before the murder. A very elderly gentleman, his name is Warwick Aston Plant and he lives in Brierley Hill. His parents and grandparents had kept a well known hostelry in High Street, Brierley Hill called the Crown. A very exclusive place it was frequented mostly by local businessmen. Not wishing to take up the family trade he went to the offices of some accountants after leaving school. His employers had offices in Bromsgrove as well as Dudley.

One day when going home for his lunch the bar was quiet as the pianist had gone for his lunch break. Warwick saw a small woman standing at the end of the bar unnoticed by his mother, who was chatting to a customer. He called his mother to serve her.

"What can I get you?" his mother asked. "Nothing thank you, I don't drink, but would you allow me to sing in here?" His mother replied that the pianist was at lunch. "I can play for myself and I will give you any money I take," replied the woman. "that's alright, you can keep the money" said the landlady.

The small woman in her poor clothes sat and played the piano to accompany her songs. It was obvious that she was a professional. After that day she came twice a week to sing in the Crown. Her favourite song was "If I were a Blackbird." She also sang in the Mitre at Stourbridge. One day when travelling on the bus to the Bromsgrove Office, Warwick saw her working in a field next to Hagley woods with a man.

His mother made a friend of the woman and when she asked her name he remembered only part of what she told them. Her father had nicknamed her Bella because from an early age she was always trying to sing. She had been looking for some cheap lodgings and eventually went to live in Birmingham Street which was then a rough area on the outskirts of Stourbridge town. Her landlord drank a lot but could be quite kind when he was sober.

When asked how she had become so down on her luck, she told them that she had been a member of a concert party on the continent. They had come to England and because of the war could not get work so had each gone their own way to survive.

On one occasion when the weather was very bad, she had arrived very wet and cold. "Go into the kitchen and put your feet up on the fender," said his mother. When they looked at her feet they saw that there were holes in her shoes. Feeling very sorry his mother gave her a pair of crepe soled shoes which she was not very fond of. They fitted and Bella was delighted with them.

Another day she arrived with a black eye and bruised face. When questioned she said that her landlord could be rough when he was drunk. She never visited them again.

"Something has happened to her... she would not have left without telling me or saying Goodbye, it is not like her," worried the landlady. "Go down to the Mitre and see if she has been in there." Warwick went twice to the Mitre. The man she lived with was pointed out to him but he did not like the look of him so made no approach. No-one knew anything about her whereabouts. The shoes which she had been given were two tone brown and cream.

Warwick joined the airforce soon afterwards but in 1944 returned on leave. Before returning, his sister brought in a copy of the Daily Sketch. "Look Warwick, isn't that one of mother's shoes?" A photograph on the front page was familiar to both of them. It was one of the many times that Webster had put out requests for anyone who could identify objects found at the scene of the murder. They were both sure that it was one of the shoes given to Bella. Warwick's sister went to the police and the paper to give their story but no-one contacted them again and nothing more was heard of the matter.

The description of the shoes changes, sometimes black, sometimes blue, and, as Warwick said, two-tone in colour. When asking for a search of this newspaper at the Collingwood newspaper library nothing was found.

When interviewed in 2005 by the T.V. team, Warwick remembered what a really nice person Bella had been.

## BLACKCOUNTRY BUGLE AND COUNTY EXPRESS

A young boy who heard of the murder remembered the mystery and later grew up to become a journalist for The Black Country Bugle. He decided to write on crime and, as the war was over, he thought that now someone may remember some vital evidence or the Police may reveal more of the story. He wrote the story again and asked if readers could add any more details. Wilfred Byford Jones of the County Express was also interested. There were many letters in reply to the request and many and varied were the contents. They came from the surrounding area and also Cornwall, Canada and other addresses from overseas. Some writers wished him to stop investigating the matter. A few writers had information about the body, and details about the skeleton. Some had very creative imaginations. There were letters which referred to Canadian and Spy connections. Some wrote on Witchcraft and Mancheism but no-one said who she was or where she came from. These letters were published and came to the attention of Mr Cogzell, awaking a memory of a T.V. programme near the end of Webster's life. He had shown a picture of the clothing and shoes, whilst asking if anyone could identify them or their owner.

# MR COGZELL AND THE MISSING SKELETON

An expert in the shoe trade, Mr Cogzell had been a shoe factor for all of his working life. At the time of the programme, he was nursing his sick wife. She died soon afterwards and he forgot about the matter until he saw the letters in the press. He contacted the journalist and told him that there was something about the shoes which Webster had shown which he could identify.

He lived in the Lye area near to a cobbler and also in the area of a sheet metal works where buckets and baths were made by women. The sharp metals often cut into the tops of shoes and with some stitching by a local cobbler they could still be worn for work. The stitches were in a particular style which was like a signature to the repairer. If Mr Cogzell could examine them they could ask where the woman came from, for she must have worked in the factory.

Contact was made with the Forensic department at Birmingham University. Webster had passed all the evidence to Dr. Griffiths, the new man. The skeleton had always been one of Webster's prize exhibits. They had no success, for the secretary continually made excuses as the doctor was constantly unavailable.

After trying for some time they decided to go in unannounced and went straight to the laboratory. When approached the Doctor

BELLA'S SHOES LEAD NOWHERE!

was very rude to them and said that there was no skeleton and no shoes. When pressed about the matter he picked up a pair of shoes from the corner and threw them to Mr Cogzell. In disgust he was told that these were definitely not the shoes which Webster had shown on T.V.

So why was Dr. Griffiths so secretive? Why was the evidence changed? Surely the skeleton was somewhere and he would have known if it had been buried. When giving a talk I met a lady who worked with Dr. Griffiths. She told me that he did not behave in that way. He was a very quiet and polite gentleman. Had he been told not to talk?

## ANNA OF CLAVERLEY

One of the letters was from a woman who signed herself Anna of Claverley. She wished them not to pursue their quest because she said that the people concerned were beyond the reach of earthly courts. So what did she really know? How could they find her? Quaester offered £100 reward and later she did agree under her own terms to meet him with a policeman in a lonely waiting room outside Wolverhampton but no photographers or other witnesses must be there.

When she arrived she looked very prosperous and had a friend with her. She disclosed that her real name was Una and originally she came from Claverley. Before the war she had married Jack Mossop and they set up home in Kenilworth. Jack worked in an aircraft factory. He liked to drink a lot and although his job was satisfactory, they were not well off.

Late in 1940 he made friends with a Dutchman called Van Ralt, who became his drinking partner. Van Ralt had lots of money to spend and soon Jack was spending a lot of money as well. He bought expensive clothes and shoes, as well as an officer's uniform although he was not in the Forces. Una was suspicious, thinking that he must be selling secrets about his work to the Dutchman. Wanting no part in this activity she parted from him.

Late in 1941 Jack came back to see her. Looking very ill and disturbed he told her that he could not sleep because he was having nightmares and it was affecting his health. He could visualise a skull looking up at him from inside a tree. In explanation he told her that Van Ralt had told him to meet him at the Lyttelton Arms in Hagley. When he arrived, Van Ralt was there with his car. He was in an argument with a Dutchwoman. He told Jack to get into the driving seat. The argument became more heated and Ralt pushed the woman into the passenger seat and told Jack to drive up Hagley Hill. The woman had slumped forward. Jack was told to turn into Hagley Wood lane and park in a lay-by opposite the entrance to the wood. Then he was made to help carry the woman's body into the woods to a hollow tree and help to squeeze her in to the hole in the trunk which was several feet from the ground. This was about 25 yards from the road. He did not know where Van Ralt went, he never saw him again. Jack deteriorated and in 1942 he died in a mental hospital in Stafford. The other woman corroborated the story and the police checked to find that it was true. Una had no idea of the identity of the Dutch woman.

## DR. MARGARET MURRAY

In 1945, another unsolved murder was reported which had taken place in Lower Quinton in the area of the Rollright Stones. Charles Walton, a hedgecutter, was said by the villagers to be a witch. He always carried a black mirror and was able to talk to the birds and wild animals. The method of killing followed the ritualistic style known as Stacsung. The Police called in any experts they could find to help them. For several years they returned to the scene of the crime on its anniversary and apart from accidentally killing a black dog, which in magic circles may have been significant, they never solved the case.

They called on Dr. Margaret Murray for advice as she was an expert on Black Magic. A well known Egyptologist, Dr. Murray was an author who wrote well into her hundredth year. She enquired if there were any other killings in the area in unusual circumstances and the police told her about Bella. She was unwilling to confirm any links with black magic, but thought that there could have been, in view of the position and completeness of the right hand. Furthermore the time of killing may have been close to the Roman festival of Lugnasdh, which had been used in early times, in the Celtic calendar and was kept by witches. Old festivals and early religious practices were sometimes taken over into the Christian year. Bella was a witch's name and the practice of putting them in trees was well known.

## PETER DOUGLAS OSBORNE

Peter's father, the brave young man who guarded the tree was waiting to return home from the continent after a most distinguished career. The process was slow so he managed to move across the continent to Holland. There he made friends with a group of Canadians who had been inspecting the records of the German Secret Service. They were also trying to find out what happened to some of our S.O.E. personnel. An office in the Hague, next door to the house where Mata Hari had lived, was full of documents which they were taking back to Canada. Douglas Osborne begged a lift with them on the boat and they swapped many stories on the way back. He told them about the unknown woman in the tree. They told him about the many spies who had worked in the area around the Midlands.

Amongst the documents they found the description of a woman which matched Bella. The same age, stature, colouring and dental formation. She had been dropped by parachute in 1941 between Kidderminster and Birmingham under cover of an air raid. Her code name had been Clara. The Abwehr records showed that five agents had been sent to England in March and April 1941 from Holland. Two were captured, two others were sent by boat and the other a woman, failed to make contact and was presumed missing, The Dutch Police could not help, for while she lived in the Midlands she never revealed her true identity.

After the war, as his young son was growing up, the Osborne family often took walks in the woods and the boy was shown the place of the murder and told the story.

Later in the sixties, there was another outbreak of the writings on the walls. Peter asked his father for details as he would have liked to write about it for posterity. He was surprised when his father refused to talk about it and forbade him to mention the subject ever again. Why did he suddenly become silent about the case? He was not the only person to do so.

In 1943, after the body was found, another policeman was bringing his family out to sleep in a small caravan opposite the wood. He was not on the case but joined in with the search to help out of interest. He, too, followed the case and talked to his young son. In later years he, too, became silent about the case and would not allow his son to talk about it.

John Simpson looks at the 50-year-old mystery of Bella in the Wych Elm

# A look back at murder

## Who did put Bella in the Wych Elm?

This has been the burning question in the minds of many Hagley residents' for more than 50 years and the murder mystery still looks likely to remain unsolved.

But at least Peter Douglas-Osborne has clues as to the identity of the victim, given to him by his father who dealt with the case as a Stourbridge Special Constable in 1940.

His conclusive evidence is dental records of a nazi officer found in the Luftwaffe Espionage Section which match up with those of the body found in the hollow tree.

Interest in the case has been generated by vandals scrawling "who put Bella in the Wych Elm" over the obelisk at Wychbury Hill - the first time the message has appeared in eight years.

Mr Douglas-Osborne said: "When Bella's body was found in the tree at Hagley Wood her right arm had been cut off and buried approximately 13 paces away.

"This is the way medieval witches were dealt with.

"Only in light of the dental records, which closely matched with the woman's, and the information that accompanied them can we realise she was a highly educated member of Hitler and Goering's occult practices.

"We can suspect she was a spy because Goering, head of the Luftwaffe, was interested in any information concerning aircraft production.

"And with Longbridge works, Rolls Royce at Derby and the RAF storage at Hartlebury, Hagley was the perfect place for all round access to the aircraft production business.

"The records also revealed the woman had been to Heidelberg and Cambridge Universities to learn perfect English and there was no further records about her after 1940."

Despite all this information, there is no evidence to suggest who was responsible for her death and their motives - could it have been witch hunters?

And who is trying to stir up the old mystery by scrawling the message Wychbury Hill?

Maybe we will never know but the mystery is certain to baffle detectives and Hagley people for years to come.

☐ ABOVE...Graffiti on the Hagley obelisk. Picture by PHIL LOACH
LEFT...Peter Douglas-Osborne

*17*

# SOME DETAILS IN THE MANY LETTERS

To perhaps jog memories and to stimulate more interest, the reporters borrowed a skeleton from the Fire Brigade and took it to the Wood, taking many photographs for another article. As they lifted it over the gate, a passing motorist nearly had a heart attack.

Some of the writers pointed to the connections with magic. Had someone been hunting for a witch and that is why they had severed her hand?

Another one wrote in defence of the gypsies. They do not believe in the devil and only use the word as an oath. Women who misbehave are usually excluded from the tribe.

Another one said that old religions were still practised in rural England with some remnants of Mancheism. Another referred to a spectral dog i.e. Odins' hound.

One letter from Toronto looked as though the writer knew a secret. It read:

"Hasn't the answer been known to those who matter for many years?

Didn't he die a year before she was found?

When the answer was found, wasn't it allowed to rest out of kindness to those, dead and alive, who were involved for the most part unwillingly in a situation that was not of their making?

Aren't these the questions you should ask?

What was the connection between Hagley Wood, Germany, Canada and Holland?

Who were the pro-nazi sympathisers in Birmingham, Wolverhampton and Stourbridge before and during the war?

Who knew the Dutch girl's man friend in Stourbridge?

Who was the Dutch girl known as Clara?

Did Clara work for Abwehr?

Did Clara drop in on her old friends in 1941?

Did Clara visit anyone in Stourbridge?

Who died insane in 1942?

Was Karl Dickenoff really a Canadian?

What did he do while he was living in Edgbaston?

What happened to the dead woman's child and who was the father?

There are those on both sides of the Atlantic and in both hemispheres who you could ask these questions but why?

There is an eternal justice beyond earthly laws."

None of the local policemen who had worked on the case could understand what the writer was getting at. They were certainly not part of a cover up. The journalist points out that those in the know and who kept the secret must have been in very powerful positions.

We would expect that now after 60 years some of the secret documents from that time could be made available.

## BOB POOLER

I was introduced to a young policeman who was writing the history of the Police Force in the area and who had given talks to various groups. He verified the evidence I had found and he was the first person to tell me that the couple had quarrelled in the Lyttelton Arms. He was the only person I could find who had seen any of the Police files. The murder was not part of his study and he could not give any more details.

Several times there have been references to the police files and on one occasion they were to be made available. However the writer was then told that the case was still open and they could not be seen. An elderly policeman at Hindlip had referred to the Official Secrets Act...

Some years ago a programme was made for Television by Stalker about the Bella mystery. There was some very good photography of the lovely scenery and woodlands in Hagley along with some more fanciful backgrounds, but as one lady who saw the programme told me "HE WAS IN THE WRONG WOOD."

Stalker based his programme in the wood behind the Hagley Monument where the graffiti is still very much in evidence. That is Wychbury wood another well known spot for covens.

## SEPTEMBER 2005 'INSIDE OUT'
## THE MIDLANDS T.V. PROGRAMME

As after 60 years many documents have been made available for inspection, the young journalist Matthew Gull hoped that he might be able to find some more facts about Bella.

The programme makers took a lot of trouble and time to investigate all the facts found so far.

The retired manager Richard Reichenbach from Lord Cobham's estate drove us around Wychbury, convinced that the area used by Stalker was correct. Sadly as we drove to the tree from the previous programme we found that vandals had set fire to a beautiful old yew tree. It had to be cut down and was lying in the woodland draped with fresh daffodils and witches' symbols. I learned afterwards that the people who meet there love the trees and this was their way of honouring the old tree.

FIFTY YEARS ON: THE RIDDLE OF THE MYSTERIOUS BODY, MUNITIONS AND MI5 . . .

# Day death went down to the woods

"IF IT wasn't for Tommy Willetts opening his big mouth, that skeleton would probably never have been found."

For 50 years police have hunted the perpetrator of a murder so hideous it rocked the West Midlands — even in the midst of war. Was it witchcraft, a German spy plot — or a crime of passion? And why did the police suddenly close their files to the Express & Star? JONATHAN LEAKE reports

*EXPRESS AND STAR 11TH NOVEMBER 1993*

We then went to the spot where Bob Hart had found the body with his friends. This was 125 yards from the Birmingham road and then about 25 yards into the wood. We had to get permission from the Hall to go there. The filming took several days. Bob Hart was not well enough to go into the woods and was interviewed at his home. Warwick was also too frail to go to the Crown public house. He told the viewers how much his family had liked Bella. Bob Pooler was also interviewed. The journalist then also walked with Peter Douglas Osborne, with his black Labrador Numi, to trace the place where his father had taken him when he was a child. He told of the later reaction of his father when he wished to write about it.

Matthew Gull also sent to Canada for more information from the files on the S.O.E. and German Abwehr war time records. Nothing was found to help with the identification of Bella.

In Birmingham reference library, he did find a reference to a spy called Clara. Could she have been Claribella? There was no record of her execution.

He also tried in several ways to gain access to the police files but they remain adamant that the case has not been closed and will not divulge any information. Matthew agreed to send on any interesting facts which may be sent to him and he has kept his word.

## DONALD Mc CORMICK

MURDER BY WITCHCRAFT was written in 1968 and published by John Long. Mr Mc Cormick writes about the murder of Charles Walton in Lower Quinton in 1945. The police could not find the murderer in that case and the villagers would give no evidence at all. It was as though there was a wall of silence for many years. The police called in Dr. Margaret Murray, an authority on the practices of Black Magic. She confirmed that there was a definite connection with magic in the murder. The man had been pinned down by a pitchfork which was set into the hedge to hold him down and slashed with his bill hook, with wounds in a cross pattern. In the village he was known as a witch, always carrying a black mirror and was able to talk to the birds and wild animals. Dr. Murray asked if any other killings in the area had been of unusual types and was given the evidence on Bella. She could not confirm that Bella was killed by a coven but agreed that some of the aspects were suspicious. The finding of the complete right hand, the burial in a tree, the supposed time of the murder near to a Roman festival of Lugnasdagh.

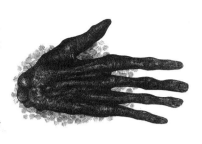

Mr McCormick looked into the evidence of spies in the area and the practices and aims of the German Abwehr and also the personnel working for Hess. As many German industrialists had visited the Midlands before the war they would have many friends who ran factories and other trades. Hess had worked on getting sympathisers and had placed personnel around the country for several years. He was a great believer in astrology and could foretell the outcomes of the war. He was convinced that Hitler would fail and his aim was to make a negotiated peace with England. Hitler also depended on the work of astrologers and other types of magic.

On one occasion his chief astrologer showed him his star chart and also one of Field Marshall Montgomery. Montgomery's was stronger so the poor man was put into prison for many years.

When Hess flew to Scotland, Hitler had one of his rages and ordered that all the astrologers and other groups were to be rounded up and killed. Many of them tried to escape. The bloodbath was called Action Hess.

Mc Cormick tried to find leads to Clara who was mentioned by Abwehr in their files. Many of the members of the Hitler and Goering circle were of course killed in the war. Some of those who did escape were trying to live secretly in places such as South America. Three men named in the files may have known something about the spy system. Otto Behne was the Gauleiter Designate for Britain after an invasion and he had spent a lot of time in Holland during the war. Kuhnemann had been the representative of a steel firm called Mannesmann visiting England, who had friends in the British Fascist Movement. A third friend of his also in the steel trade made trips to the

Midlands before the war. It is likely that they may have tried to enlist sympathisers for the Nazi cause. The only man to be tracked down was Herr Franz Rathgeb, by then living under an alias in Paraguay, retired and trying to forget his past. When approached, he was very nervous until the writer told him he was only trying to find out the identity of the skeleton.

Before the war he visited the Midlands a lot and also South Wales to sell steel. Yes, he had tried to find some people who might be sympathetic but he was mostly interested in trade not politics.

He had known of an agent named Lehrer who lived with a Dutch woman in Germany. Before the war, she lived in Birmingham. She was well educated and intelligent and her height and description fitted, as well as her irregular teeth which marred her otherwise attractive appearance. Rathgeb could not remember her name but it would have probably been an alias anyway. She did know a lot about Birmingham and the locations of the big factories. Her memory for maps was exceptional and she knew that in case of war there were plans to evacuate some of the major factories. She had links with England at least up to 1939. another thing was the talk of an unhappy affair with a man in Stourbridge. He recalled that town, for it was a place which he had once visited. He was told that she came from Utrecht but she may have been part German and posed as Dutch, in order to infiltrate the resistance. The last time he saw her was at the end of a party when she was reading horoscopes. In 1941 things became very difficult so she may have been killed in an air raid or rounded up by Action Hess. It had not been a safe time to ask questions.

No files had reported her missing although a woman had been parachuted during an air raid between Kidderminster and Birmingham. No British reports were found of a spy caught or executed with her description, then or later.

Many people did believe in the power of astrology on both sides. When invasion looked imminent many astrologers banded together to exert their power over Hitler's thoughts to stop him. The same thing happened when Napoleon waited on the other side of the channel.

## SOME INTERESTING CONNECTIONS TO THE STORY ANDREW BULLAS

After the T.V. programme was shown on 9th September 2005, an old friend brought a message from her son. Andrew is a film maker for the War Museum and works in Cambridge. He is also a writer who produced a play about the Bella mystery for T.V., which is very good but has not yet been produced. He was kind enough to send me a copy.

"Why didn't she mention the Gateacre connection?" he asked his mother. They knew that sometime in 1941 the then Squire Gateacre suddenly left the great Hall which was his home, taking nothing with him and leaving the house open. He did not return for many years. During that time the house was stripped and vandalised (it was in poor condition anyway). The Squire was a second son who had not expected to inherit the title, but his brother was killed in the Great War. He came back from Canada with his Canadian wife, to live in a house which needed repairs and an estate impoverished by death duties. He was not a popular man in the village as he did not live up to the expectations of the villagers' idea of a squire. He drank heavily and was a womaniser. He was also always short of money. After the sad death of a child, his wife left him and returned to Canada. It was said that he was the father of an illegitimate child. Soon the old hall had been emptied and the Park was used as an American base. These are the stories about the man but the villagers would not talk about the matter, there was another veil of silence.

Andrew also later sent me some cuttings about a spy who was found dead in an air raid shelter in Cambridge. This matched the death of Karl Dickenoff as described in the book Murder by Witchcraft but I do not know whether it was the same man. The details were interesting for it showed how devious the Germans were. This man had letters sent from England, to families still in Germany, through the Red Cross. With these he could blackmail people into helping him as he knew where their families lived, so they could be murdered. We shall never know how many people may have helped the Germans against their will. This type of embarrassment could be a reason for keeping secret such happenings and for not opening the case. I learned a little more about the interesting Squire later.

## JUDITH O'DONOVAN

Matthew Gull kindly promised to let me know if any other information came to him. He later gave me the telephone number of Judith who lived locally so that we could meet and talk together. Judith had been brought up in Claverley and remembered seeing the Hall when it was empty with some of the books etc. lying on the floor of the library. The house was in a very poor state.

During the war, her parents often visited the village Inn at weekends, there was little other entertainment then. Her father was a cousin of Jack Mossop. He. was often there drinking with a Dutchman called Van Ralt. The Squire was often in the same group and also women It was not unusual for fights to break out. To the surprise of the village Jack Mossop began to dress in very expensive clothes and shoes. He also had an R.A.F. officer's uniform although he was not in the forces but still worked in an aircraft factory. His wages would not have paid for such luxuries and clothes were difficult to obtain then. People became suspicious.

Later in 1941 Jack visited his grandmother who had brought him up. He was very frightened and asked her to give him money so that he could escape but the old lady was poor and could not help him. His illness became more severe and he was taken into a mental hospital in Stafford where he died in 1942. Van Ralt was not seen in the village again. Suddenly the Squire left his house in a most unusual way. He left after breakfast leaving the house unlocked and leaving everything without telling anyone. The house was soon stripped and as it was already in poor repair became sadly neglected with the roof open to the skies. The villagers were unwilling to discuss the mystery. It was known that the squire had an illegitimate child but no-one revealed who the mother was.

In later years the squire did return to live in a small house until his death. He married a lady from Clent who only left him one penny in her will. Was there a family connection in Clent as a Miss Gateacre lived in Clent House in the early 30s?

Judith obtained a copy of the death certificate of Jack Mossop. He was still quite a young man. He died from an overdose of drugs. Did he steal them to take his own life? Or were they administered to get him out of the way?

Dutch soldiers were billeted near to Claverley. The Dutch resistance was used by spies to get into England.

The fact that the woman slumped forward when pushed into the car was also of interest. The secret army was allowed to kill any persons who may have put our country in jeopardy. This was sometimes carried out by a poisoned needle bringing on a heart attack soon after use. Jack only referred to the quarrel as heated and did not specify a violent attack by Van Ralt. There may have been families who later could be hurt to find out the deeds carried out by parents or relatives in the war under orders for the defence of the realm. Many brave young men were ready to risk their lives for us in case of an invasion. Many deeds, whether legal or criminal, could have taken place at such a time when it would have been unwise to see or know too much about what was going on.

If we had been invaded many of us may not have behaved as bravely as we hope we would.

As for Bella, despite the twists and turns of all the investigations carried out by police, journalists and others interested in the case, her murder remains unsolved.